Seconds, Minutes, and Hours

Holly Karapetkova

Vero Beach, Florida 32964

www.rourkepublishing.com

PHOTO CREDITS: © gbrundin: Title Page, 12; © Nikada: 3; © Larisa Lofitskaya: 5; © Kim Gunkel: 6, 22; © Donna Coleman: 7; © Reuban Shulz: 9; © Luis Carlos Torres: 9; © andy lim: 10, 22, 23; © kate sept2004: 11; © Jose Manuel Gelpi Diaz: 13; © bonnie jacobs: 14, 23; © Aldo Murillo: 15; ©John Clines: page 17; © Ozgur Donmaz: 18; © Rob Belknap: 19, 23; © Zoran Mircetic: 20; © Daniel R. Burch: 20; © VisualField: 21; © agencyby: 21; © ronen: 21; © Jim Jurica: 21

Editor: Meg Greve

Cover design by Nicola Stratford, bdpublishing.com

Interior Design by Heather Botto

Library of Congress Cataloging-in-Publication Data

Karapetkova, Holly.
    Seconds, minutes, and hours / Holly Karapetkova.
        p. cm. -- (Concepts)
    ISBN 978-1-60694-379-3 (hard cover)
    ISBN 978-1-60694-511-7 (soft cover)
    ISBN 978-1-60694-569-8 (bilingual)
    1. Time--Juvenile literature. I. Title.
    QB209.5.K375 2010
    529'.7--dc22
                                2009015991

Printed in the USA

CG/CG

www.rourkepublishing.com - rourke@rourkepublishing.com
Post Office Box 643328 Vero Beach, Florida 32964

Seconds, minutes, and hours help us measure time.

3

A second is very short.

What can you do in a second?

I can wink.

I can snap.

A minute is longer than a second.

What can you do in a minute?

60 seconds = 1 minute

I can write my name.

I can count to 50.

An hour is longer than
a minute.
What can you do in an hour?

60 minutes = 1 hour

I can play in a soccer game.

I can go to the library.

A day is longer than an hour. What can you do in a day?

24 hours = 1 day

MONTH_____ YEAR_____

SUNDAY	MONDAY	TUESDAY	WEDNESDAY	THURSDAY	FRIDAY	SATURDAY

I can visit my grandma.

I can go to school.

What do we use to measure time?

clock

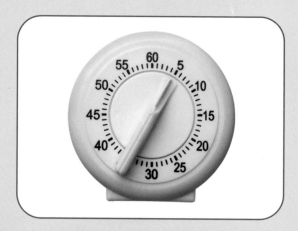

kitchen timer

stopwatch

hourglass

watch

digital clock

Converting Time

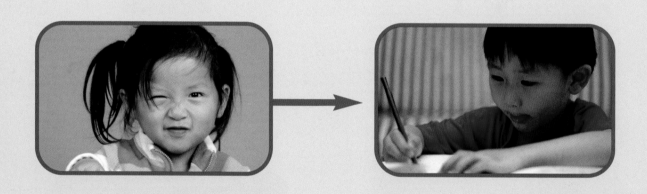

60 seconds = 1 minute

60 minutes = 1 hour

24 hours = 1 day

Index

Websites to Visit

www.ictgames.com/hickory4.html

www.crickweb.co.uk/assets/resources/flash.php?&file=Toolkit%20index2a

www.bbc.co.uk/schools/digger/5_7entry/4.shtml

www.time-for-time.com/swf/myclox.swf

www.netrover.com/~kingskid/timeindex1.htm

gokidding.com/time.htm

About the Author

Holly Karapetkova, Ph.D., loves writing books and poems for kids and adults. She teaches at Marymount University and lives in the Washington, D.C., area with her son K.J. and her two dogs, Muffy and Attila.